Make your church's money work:

Achieving financial integrity in your congregation

John Temple

©Day One Publications 2008
First printed 2008

A CIP record is held at the British Library

ISBN 978-1-84625-150-4

Published by Day One Publications, Ryelands Road, Leominster, HR6 8NZ
☎ 01568 613 740
FAX 01568 611 473
email—sales@dayone.co.uk
web site—www.dayone.co.uk
North American email—usasales@dayone.co.uk

Cover designed by Wayne McMaster and printed by Gutenberg Press, Malta

588

120320

COMMENDATIONS

In the UK especially, there are far too few books on church finance—especially ones that begin with the conviction that vision should always take precedence over money. This daring yet simple concept alone could well begin a revolution in evangelical church life if taken seriously. John Temple's book—often provocative, sometimes controversial—clearly explains why this is so and uses biblical principles, personal examples and a healthy dose of common sense to do so, as well as giving many practical examples of how church finances could be managed. Few treasurers and leadership teams will fail to benefit from a careful consideration of the principles set out here.

Gary Benfold, Pastor, Moordown Baptist Church, Bournemouth, England

A failure to establish biblically derived financial policies and practices often leads churches into trouble. Following this eminently practical guide should ensure that both God and his servants are honoured in this vital area and that much potential difficulty and heartache are avoided. Supremely qualified to write on this subject, John Temple is a peerless conveyor of sanctified common sense. I heartily commend this little volume.

Jonathan Stephen, Director, Affinity, and Principal, WEST (Wales Evangelical School of Theology)

In a simple yet authoritative fashion, John Temple has constructed the framework for a church financial management system intended to energize the local church's vision and enhance the global church's witness. Make Your Church's Money Work *is comprehensive but concise, and easy to read, understand and execute by clergy and laity alike. Its biblical foundation ensures its value and the personal illustrations demonstrate its practicality as a blueprint for fidelity to God and his gospel. If you're new to Christian ministry or church membership,* Make Your Church's Money Work *will set a biblical benchmark for your ministry or life. If you're seasoned in Christianity, it will make you wish you could begin again, with this book as your guide.* Make Your Church's Money Work *is of inestimable worth but, at its inexpensive cost, every church should possess multiple copies to be read by church members and especially those directly engaged in managing church finances.*

Dr Reggie Weems, Senior Pastor, Heritage Baptist Church, Johnson City, Tennessee, USA

At last! Take a thorough knowledge of scriptural teaching, sprinkle it liberally with years of hands-on experience in the local church, and you have what you are holding in your hands! Here is a book worth far more than its slim weight: an easy read, yet an invaluable resource for church leaders and members who want to be even more faithful in their stewardship. This would be one of the ten books I would give to a pastor starting out in ministry or to a church with a passion for Christ's kingdom.

Roland Eskinazi, Pastor of Goodwood Baptist Church, Cape Town, South Africa

ACKNOWLEDGEMENTS

Early in the 1970s, my wife and I, together with a number of friends, became exercised about the *application* of sound theology to practical aspects of our lives. At that time, we were in the process of establishing the Lynnwood Baptist Church in Pretoria, South Africa. We realized that it would be hypocritical to teach members of the congregation to follow the Bible in all aspects of their lives but not to apply the same standards to the church itself. We therefore wrestled with church organization, administration and finance. Could we make the Bible the starting point for all of these practical aspects of church life? The outcome in the financial realm was something along the lines of what is described in this book. I acknowledge the patience of the early congregation at Lynnwood and, subsequently, in another church plant at Newlands in Cape Town. These Bible-minded people helped frame our policies and practices, and contributed greatly to the views which I express in this book.

My appreciation to the reviewers of this work, namely Brian Edwards, who also wrote the Foreword, Reggie Weems, Jonathan Stephen and Gary Benfold, who also contributed editorial comment.

Finally, my special appreciation to Suzanne Mitchell, for editing the work in true professional style.

John Temple
August 2008

CONTENTS

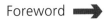

FOREWORD

Money matters in the life of the Christian, but even more so in the life of the church; unfortunately, too many congregations are irresponsible, irrational and even illegal in the way they handle their income and expenditure. With a watching world and ever-tighter legal requirements, it is essential that both leaders and members should behave financially in ways that are 'above reproach'.

John Temple is not only a businessman with many years at the helm of various companies—experience that does not automatically qualify anyone to write on the subject of church finance—he is also a Christian committed to allowing the precepts, principles and precedents of the Bible to govern every area of life. In this, he insists, the church is not exempt. After a lifetime of rigorously applying the Word of God to his own business life (see his *Be Successful, Be Spiritual*, Day One Publications), John turns his attention to the financial affairs of a local Christian community and applies the same strong biblical criteria. His long involvement in church planting and leadership also qualifies him to deal with this subject. With practical application and insight the author covers a wide range of issues, from stewardship to budgeting, salaries and a host of details besides.

I have been privileged to count John and his wife Yvonne as personal friends for many years, and I know that their financial control in the home, in business and wherever they have had church responsibility is conducted with absolute integrity, Christian motivation and a strict application of what God teaches. Every church leader and responsible member should read *Make Your Church's Money Work*.

Brian H. Edwards
Surbiton, 2008

Introduction

... aim at what is honourable not only in the Lord's sight but also in the sight of man.

–2 Cor. 8:21

Some years ago, my wife and I attended a sound evangelical church where the notices included an apology that details of the offering from the previous week could not be given because it had been stolen before it could be counted! The church was situated in a rough part of a city, but we were still a bit shocked. We were even more shocked when, on our next visit, the same apology appeared again. I hoped that this church had adequate insurance to cope with this type of problem; nevertheless, it reinforced my long-held view that good stewardship of the church's finances demands a sound administration structure and sensible procedures.

This book is therefore intended to be a guide for all who seek to establish and maintain integrity in church finances or give money to the church. It should be read by all church leaders, but also by those who are interested in sound administration, spend any of the church's money or give money to a church. The church's money is the Lord's money and needs to be handled with a measure of care which *exceeds* that with which we handle our own money.

I have had the privilege of worshipping in many churches on five continents. Most of these congregations hold to the same Bible-based evangelical teaching, yet they differ substantially in many organizational and practical details. How is this possible? Quite simply because the Bible leaves us with a fair amount of freedom to function in accordance with our particular situations without compromising any theological *principles*. For practical reasons, churches must make decisions on how they will plan and organize their finances. They need guidance on how best to do this. The Bible does not present a blueprint for financial details, but it is not entirely silent either. It does give guidance, and we need to rank the importance of what we may or may not do, always starting with the Bible. I suggest that four levels of guidance exist in the Bible:

Precepts
These are summarized in the Ten Commandments and are the overarching laws against which everything must be measured.

Principles
These are further specific biblical laws which must be observed by the New Testament church. They will be found in the teaching portions, notably in the epistles, the Gospels and sometimes in Acts.

Precedents
These are historic records found in the Bible which are excellent examples and should be followed as good practice. Precedents are to be found in the historic records of the New Testament, for example, in portions of the Gospels, Acts and sometimes even in the epistles. We would expect all precedents to be examples of the principles set out in the teaching portions, and this is indeed what we find.

Freedoms
These are guidelines which may be inferred from Scripture (or from Scripture's silence) and can be determined through Spirit-led wisdom. Freedoms may never be in conflict with any precept or principle. Thus we enjoy a certain amount of freedom, leaving us with scope to introduce many theologically neutral variations into church practice. These practices are to be determined with the aid of Spirit-led common sense and following prayer. In this book I will be giving specific examples of freedoms that have been tested in churches over many years. Freedom should not,

however, be confused with autonomy, in which each person is free simply to do as he pleases.

Let me illustrate these points. In 2 Corinthians 8, Paul describes how the Macedonian church had collected money for the relief of the poor in Jerusalem, and he encourages the Corinthians to do the same. Then he goes on to describe how the churches have appointed Titus (an elder) plus another reputable brother to accompany the party (including Paul) to deliver the money in Jerusalem, explaining, 'We take this course so that no one should blame us about this generous gift that is being administered by us, for we aim at what is honourable not only in the Lord's sight but also in the sight of man' (vv. 20–21). Here we have a *precedent*, or historic record, of what the early church did. We would do well to follow the examples of these churches, but we stop short of making these actions *principles*. However, buried in the text, Paul does go on to teach a *principle*, namely that of being 'honourable' in the sight of God and of man. In the arena of freedom, Paul points out that the churches are employing the well established culture of the day (based on Old Testament *principle*), namely of using two or more witnesses. In our time, perhaps this means two signatories on all cheques. We will come back to this principle later. Finally, we see the *freedom* exercised by the church in selecting the man who is to accompany Paul.

Some churches will be blessed with members skilled in accounting or finance. That is a good start, but such people must be encouraged to adapt their thinking to *what is needed in a church*. The above illustration from 2 Corinthians demonstrates why it is necessary for them to satisfy the prevailing culture embodied in the applicable accounting standards and laws, but they must also never lose sight of the purpose of accounting to the church. It differs from an organization which seeks to make a profit or accumulate assets. The church has spiritual goals, and sound accounting must primarily serve these goals.

The treasurer, operating in submission to the leadership, must guide the church both in the principles on which the church finances are to be based and in the budgeted amounts which are clearly in the arena of *freedoms*. This also means that the leadership must carry the church with it, which in turn demands clear, simple, adequate communication, *free from accounting jargon*. Reporting must also be carried out diligently. Suppose, for example, that a donation is made for a specific purpose or ministry. The people involved need to know about it as soon as possible so that they can get on with their planning and implementation.

One of the key messages of this book is that we must do things 'decently and in order' (1 Cor. 14:40). We must also 'render to Caesar the things that are Caesar's' (Matt. 22:21), implying scrupulous adherence to the laws of the country in which our churches are located, provided that those laws are *not in conflict with the Bible*. I will not attempt to list these requirements, not even for the countries with which I am familiar. The reason is twofold. Firstly, this book is not about man's laws, but about God's laws and some practical ideas for practising integrity before God in the matter of church finances. Secondly, the laws of every country change continuously and anything that I write now will soon be out of date. I therefore recommend that churches contact their denominational or association office, which will doubtless be able to advise them on the latest laws and reporting requirements. Professional accountants or lawyers should have little difficulty coming to grips with the reporting and legal demands. It is possible for churches to be operating in good faith but in conflict with the laws of the country. Care must be taken to ensure that the witness of the church is not damaged by such unintentional actions.

I will avoid dealing with the issue of church government in order to make this book as applicable as possible to all evangelical churches regardless of denomination or form of church government. I am fully aware of the differences between the congregational government based on democracy and those forms which centralize control. My own position falls short of full democracy, as it appears nowhere in the Bible, but I am assuming some measure of approval by the congregation. This will be somewhat at odds with churches that centralize decision-making in the eldership or church council, and sometimes even with very large churches where congregational rule becomes impractical. The only New Testament precedent that we have on this issue is found in Acts 6, where the proposals of the apostles resulted in the words, 'And what they said pleased the whole gathering' (Acts 6:5). Quite how this 'pleasing' was determined we are not told; it may have been by a vote or simply the assessment of the mood of the people by the apostles. Whatever method was used, we note that the decision resulted in the church prospering thereafter. In the realm of freedoms, spiritual results are a good indication of the quality of a decision. You will therefore note that in budgeting, I assume involvement and approval by the congregation. How this is achieved may differ from church to church; this is a matter of freedom. Indeed, some churches will not even bring the budget to the wider congregation, preferring to have the elders, deacons or a church council approve the budget and the accounts. I still regard this as 'church approval', because when a person joins such a church, he or she acknowledges this form of government. Presbyterians and others who practise this form of government should therefore understand 'church approval' to include whichever form they have decided to follow.

Stewardship

Chapter 1

Moreover, it is required of stewards that they be found trustworthy.

−1 Cor. 4:2

tewardship is part of God's grace. He entrusted the world to us without us deserving any of it. The world does not belong to us but is loaned to us for safekeeping, growth and enjoyment. This concept is rooted in creation, part of the account of which reads, 'The LORD God took the man and put him in the garden of Eden to *work it and keep it*' (Gen. 2:15, emphasis added). The NIV puts it, 'take care of it'. God also entrusted the gospel to us and, by extension, the growth and development of the church. The entire series of which this book is part is essentially about the stewardship of the church. This book focuses on the stewardship of the church and its members in the use of their money in order to promote the gospel and build up the church.

Stewardship in the Bible literally meant 'management of a household' (or 'the law over the house'), in much the same way in which the slave Joseph managed the home of Potiphar. This is a good picture, since it is the same in the household of the church. We are to manage the church so that the gospel may flourish in every aspect. Just as a slave owned none of the things that he or she managed, so *we own no part of the church*, even if we happen to be the largest, or even the only, donor. Stewards were mostly slaves in New Testament times and were sometimes referred to as 'servants'. We should all see ourselves as 'servants', however influential we may be. (For more on stewardship, the reader is referred to a website which offers resources covering the subject from the time of the Puritans to the present day.[1])

Jesus commended faithfulness (or trustworthiness) in the parable of the servant who used the talents entrusted to him to fulfil the owner's best interests: 'His master said to him, "Well done, good and *faithful* servant. You have been faithful over a little; I will set you over much. Enter into the joy of your master"' (Matt. 25:21, emphasis added). Paul stated plainly, 'Moreover, it is required of stewards that they be found *trustworthy*' (1 Cor. 4:2, emphasis added). These commands are applicable to everyone, but the elders, and the treasurer in particular, *must* practise sound stewardship. This means taking great care in spending money at every level in the church. There should be no extravagance, no waste and no investing in the egos or personal satisfaction of any of the people involved. I will expand on this last point.

In his Devotional Bible, Spurgeon wrote: 'Faithfulness is a great virtue. Whatever may happen to us, we must be exact to a farthing in the keeping of accounts. A Christian should be one whom all can trust with untold gold. Whether we are household servants, or lords of the land, our first duty to our fellow man is scrupulous honesty.'[2]

Most churches have members with a variety of skills and it is valuable to have them use those gifts in *the service of the church*. However, it is possible for these same people to use the *church in the service of their gifts*! Let me illustrate. Suppose a gifted concert pianist offers to play for the church. He claims that, in order to realize his full potential as a pianist and to allow the church to sing properly to the glory of God, he needs a Steinway grand piano. So the church buys it for him and he plays it expansively at every opportunity. This musician is really *using the church* as playing practice or possibly even as an audience to further his concert-playing ambitions. Is this good stewardship? Would it not be preferable to buy a piano which is good value for money and properly cared for? The first priority of a church pianist (or any other musician) is to lead the singing so as to glorify God. Check this principle in *every ministry* and *every item* that the church purchases. All workers should also check their own motives. I am not suggesting that churches buy the cheapest equipment nor do things badly. I am pleading for good 'stewardship', and for gifted members not to use the church to satisfy their personal ambitions.

Many years ago, I was involved in the planting of a church, so I took my family on several trips to various churches in the USA to learn something about church growth. In at least one of these churches, I was surprised at the emphasis placed on the building. Most church buildings I visited were excellent and served the purpose well. One was magnificent, and I wondered what the motivation had been to raise and spend so much money on something way beyond what was needed. Was it to glorify God and demonstrate to the world that the congregation really cared about its congregation rather than the building? Or was it the self-aggrandizement of the leadership? I was in the process of erecting our new church building and I realized how easily I could use it to live out my personal ambitions and seek to attract praise and appreciation for my efforts. We must examine our motives when we build, refurbish or modernize our church buildings. I am keen on having a good, modern and functional building. I am also keen on using all the modern technology that is available to ensure that the gospel is heard properly and that we sing well to God's glory. But I am against doing these things to fulfil any personal ambition, be it on the part of the leaders or of any member of the congregation. James condemns selfish ambition, saying, 'For where jealousy and selfish ambition exist, there will be disorder and every vile practice' (James 3:16).

Transparency

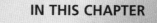

Chapter 2

For nothing is hidden except to be made manifest;
nor is anything secret except to come to light.

–Mark 4:22

Before we get into the details of how to organize the finances of a church, we need to grasp a key principle. I shall call it the 'principle of transparency'. Put simply, it is the old adage of not only *doing* right but also being *seen* to be doing right. This principle is so important that it is worth repeating. We go back to Paul writing to the Corinthians about carrying the collection to Jerusalem:

> With him [Titus] we are sending the brother who is famous among all the churches for his preaching of the gospel. And not only that, but he has been appointed by the churches to travel with us as we [including Paul] carry out this act of grace that is being ministered by us, for the glory of the Lord himself and to show our good will. *We take this course so that no one should blame us* about this generous gift that is being administered by us, for we aim at what is honourable *not only in the Lord's sight but also in the sight of man.* And with them we are sending our brother whom we have often *tested and found earnest* in many matters, but who is now more earnest than ever because of his great confidence in you.
>
> 2 Cor. 8:18–22, emphasis added

No less a person than the apostle Paul was carrying the money, yet he deemed it necessary to be accompanied by an esteemed elder, Titus, *plus* two other unnamed brothers, one of whom had been 'often tested and found earnest'. Paul knew that in God's sight they would be faithful in delivering the money, but he also wanted the people to *see* that they had been faithful. Possibly the other three were required to report back.

There are also many Old Testament precedents from which we can learn. Just one example illustrates this point. In Ezra 8, we read how Ezra made the Levites weigh all the silver and gold vessels before the Jews left for Jerusalem and then, when they arrived, they checked the weight again. Ezra makes this point: 'The total was counted and weighed, and the weight of everything was recorded' (Ezra 8:34). Sound accounting is an ancient biblical practice.

We are under the same obligation now. In Paul's time, 'seeing' was accomplished by taking along additional men of excellent reputation, and in Ezra's time, it involved weighing the vessels before twelve of the leading priests. We must ask ourselves what it takes in our age to ensure that the congregation 'sees' that the leaders behave with integrity. Let me give some practical examples:

- The treasurer must present clear and meaningful budgets and reports to the church on a regular basis. Reports may need to be given to ministry leaders even more frequently. These must include sufficient detail to avoid any suspicion of items being hidden or 'slipped through', but must also be sufficiently summarized so as not to confuse non-financial people. It is up to the church to decide whether this should take place monthly, quarterly or annually. In our day, 'see' probably means doing a PowerPoint presentation! This form of reporting is one of the key tasks of the treasurer.

- The treasurer must follow the current accounting standards and legal demands in reporting the financial affairs to whichever authority requires reports. (In the UK, these will be the charity laws, revenue laws, and the accepted accounting standards of the day). Reports should be subject to independent checking (or auditing if this is required) and be scrupulously transparent. Rules on 'related-party' transactions (doing business with people who are linked to the church or the leaders) must be observed. These reports will not, however, satisfy the principle of transparency *within the church*, because the congregation is unlikely to understand the accounting jargon and the layout used. These reports are also unlikely to highlight the key issues which are of real interest to the church.

In my experience, the above practices are commonplace, but sometimes the entire process falls down because there is no transparency at the *source* of income, namely at the counting of the offering. The church income is the *largest single amount* in the church accounts, yet it is often not subject to any independent verification! I am told that, in some churches, the offering is simply bagged and taken home to be counted later by the treasurer. I cannot believe that this is legal in any country. At the other extreme, some churches contract independent banks to collect the offering, count it in the presence of church officers acting as witnesses and then take it to the bank in an armoured vehicle! The income of most churches does not merit this level of security, but the principles remain the same regardless of size. My advice to treasurers is to have two people, other than him- or herself, count the offering *in a place where the congregation can observe it being done* (in one church to which I belonged, it was counted on the communion table), then record the income in duplicate and have the record signed by both members in addition to the treasurer or his/her nominee. One copy goes with the money for banking (he or she then generates a paper trail that this has happened), and the other is kept (preferably in a safe) as a record. In the event of a loss, this record will also be the basis of an insurance claim. Churches need to protect themselves, and the treasurer needs to protect his or her own reputation. What would Paul have done in our times?

The same principles, suitably adapted, should be followed for all sources of income. Clearly, bank cheques received in the post or direct debits into the bank account can—and should be— verified by the external auditor.

Expense claims must likewise be transparent and signed by the person making the claim as well as the one (usually the treasurer) authorized to approve the amount. All expenditures should be against supporting invoices which clearly describe the product or service. The principle should be followed so that, in the event of anyone checking on a single item of expenditure, it must be easy to prove that it was legitimately spent on the item described and was authorized by the right person in the church. All payments should be made only by cheque or verifiable bank transfers so that payments can be audited later.

This may sound like a lot of bureaucracy, but it is necessary in order to maintain integrity in the 'sight of men'. We have already noted the huge effort that Paul went to in this regard (2 Cor. 8:18–22). Travel in his day was difficult, tedious and, no doubt, expensive. The people who were chosen for that particular task were also valuable members of their congregations (one was Titus; another was 'famous … for his preaching'!). Yet Paul deemed all of this worthwhile in order to be transparent before men, even though God knew the truth.

Budgeting and financial control

For which of you, desiring to build a tower, does not first sit down and count the cost?

–Luke 14:28

This may seem like a technical subject reserved for the church treasurer and those few people in the church who understand financial matters, but it is not. The budget of the church is a real practical expression of where the priorities of the church lie. It embodies the vision of the church (a spiritual matter) and should be led by the elders and understood and supported by the entire congregation (or whatever constitutes the decision-making body of the church). Is budgeting (i.e. financial planning) biblical? The Bible does not spell it out, but Jesus did use the example of planning in his comments on counting the cost of becoming a disciple: 'For which of you, desiring to build a tower, does not first sit down and count the cost, whether he has enough to complete it?' (Luke 14:28). It is inconceivable that Jesus would have used such an example had the answer to his rhetorical question been 'No one'. Consider also the building of the temple in the Old Testament:

> … for the altar of incense made of refined gold, and its weight; also *his plan* for the golden chariot of the cherubim that spread their wings and covered the ark of the covenant of the Lord. All this he made clear to me in writing from the hand of the Lord, all the *work to be done according to the plan.*
>
> 1 Chr. 28:18–19, emphasis added

Notice that God produced the plan and that it was *in writing*! Dare we be less meticulous than God himself?

Living out the vision and presenting a challenge
Most churches will readily explain what they see to be their

major tasks. Generally, these will include such noble aims as spreading the gospel and building up the believers. Churches often include other commendable aims such as supporting missions, alleviation of poverty, contributing to the community and so on. Some churches are blessed with leaders of great vision and they present these aims as challenges to the church. They encourage the church members to give and work, thereby living out the vision of the church.

This is all fine, but how can you determine whether a church really means to do what it says it plans to do? Very simply by looking at its annual budget! The priorities of the church will be reflected in where the money will go. If, for example, a church says that one of its primary tasks is evangelism, but only a small fraction of its budget goes on evangelism, is it being consistent? Is it even being honest?

The budget is therefore the means by which the elders, supported by the church, demonstrate their commitment to their declared aims. Consequently, it should be developed with as much participation as possible from the members. It must also be presented in simple, non-accounting terms, without, of course, undermining any accounting rules. How can this be achieved?

Before we get into details of the budget itself, we should observe some very valuable precedents set out in Acts 6:1–6. We would do well to follow these examples of behaviour. The apostles were in trouble with the wider congregation and were required to exercise leadership in a practical matter. The congregation was 'grumbling'. Does this sound familiar? The apostles did not shirk their responsibility but called the congregation together and then *they* (the apostles or leaders) proposed a solution— in other words, they *led*. Precedent number one: the *leaders* proposed a solution. Precedent number two: the *congregation* approved through some means or other. Precedent number three: the congregation was 'pleased'. The members arrived grumbling but went away happy! All those leading in the church should aim not merely for acquiescence or to solve the problem, but also to *please* as many members as possible (never forgetting that our primary duty is to please God first). We should not give up easily on this aim.

As explained in the Introduction, this book does not explain church government in any detail and readers may consult several good books on this subject.[3] Here I am simply assuming that a church is led by elders, even if your church calls them by a different name. One of the tasks of the elders is to set direction as well as ensure that the aims of the church are realized. Therefore, at the outset of the budgeting process, the church must decide where it is going or what it intends achieving. This is its 'vision'. It answers the practical questions: What ministries will it include in its programme? Will there be a Sunday school? A Bible school? A missions programme? Outreach? Men's ministry? Women's ministry? Seniors' ministry? Youth ministry? Building development? Church planting? Social concern? The list is potentially very long. It must be developed and prioritized by the elders so that the plans can be implemented *as the Lord provides*. This programme is then ideally supported by the church and the persuasion process should continue until it pleases as many people as possible. Once the overall vision is set, the church can progress to the budget process, because all ministries inevitably require funding. Whichever form of government is practised at your church, members of your congregation will ultimately vote with their money and then with their feet! They will either stay and cheerfully support the vision and practice of the church, or they will leave.

We now move to the details of the budgeting process. Note that this is in the realm of freedom. Common sense and prayer will be the underlying techniques in this area. I suggest here a budgeting process which fits into the above-mentioned principles, draws on the precedents, makes accounting and business sense and, above all, is not in conflict with any biblical principles. But do not forget the prayer part!

Budgeting process

I will assume that the church has settled on a number of ministries or departments and that each is, ideally, led by a deacon working under an elder, who, in turn, is under the entire eldership. This deacon will co-ordinate a team of workers whose job it will be to implement the vision of the church as it relates to that particular ministry. The purpose of the budgeting process is to determine how much each ministry—and then, by implication, the church—needs to spend in the forthcoming year.

All departments must be asked prayerfully and responsibly to calculate their needs and forward them to the treasurer, who may possibly be a deacon or even an elder. The treasurer will then consolidate all departmental budgets and add those parts under his or her control so as to produce a 'unified' (or 'consolidated') church budget. This proposed budget must then be presented to the elders for approval, and finally to the church. The key issue is to check that the aims of the church are fairly represented in the various budget allocations.

It is worth pausing here. Some churches allow individual departments to run autonomous budgets, bank accounts and accounts. Since we are in the realm of freedoms, we cannot reject this process altogether. However, the authorities in some countries will require consolidated accounts for the entire church which they (the authorities) will assume are under the trusteeship of a common leadership. Trying to achieve this with various autonomous budgets and accounts becomes complicated. Furthermore, the ability to budget, appeal for income and report for the entire church is also made more difficult. Finally, I also think that a biblical principle lies just below the surface. Paul calls on us to submit to one another 'out of reverence for Christ' (Eph. 5:21), and the writer to the Hebrews calls on us to submit to our leaders: 'Obey your leaders and submit to them, for they are keeping watch over your souls, as those who will have to give an account. Let them do this with joy and not with groaning, for that would be of no advantage to you' (Heb. 13:17). Notice that in this work it is the turn of the *leaders* to be joyful *while the members submit*! Surely this is best implemented by producing a unified budget to which all are in submission? This will call for some members, who do not agree, to 'submit' to the leadership of the elders and, in congregational churches, to the general will of the church.

What if the budget produced in this way is considered to be unrealistic? I will deal with faith later, but at some point the elders and then the church will have to come to terms with what they consider to be a responsible budget within their *faith*, but not within their *resources*. This process can be aided by dividing the operating expenses into two groups, namely 'non-discretionary' and 'discretionary' expenditure. Non-discretionary items are those which *must* be paid, such as utility bills, the pastor's salary, essential accommodation costs and so on. Other items, defined as 'discretionary', can be budgeted on the basis of only spending the money *if and when* it becomes available. Clearly the line between the two types of expenditure is a matter for prayerful determination in each church.

So far, I have been dealing with the expenses side of the budget. What about the income? The bulk of the income should come in the form of the offerings or donations. However, some ministries will attract income either in the form of subscriptions or sales (e.g. sale of books, CDs or DVDs); other ministries will appeal to the particular interest of a donor. The latter is referred to as a 'restricted' or 'specified' donation and the church can only use such income to pay expenses under that heading. This really is no problem and merely requires that the income budget be broken up into these different classes. Consider the example of a person who has a burden for missions and places an envelope marked 'missions' in the offering bag. This goes into the 'missions' income line of the accounts and *must* be used for missions and only missions. If more comes into the missions budget than is spent in any one year, the surplus cannot be used for anything else, but must either be spent in that year or carried forward into the following year for missions. The same is true for all specified or restricted income.

In Appendix 1, I offer a model budget which can be adapted for use in any church. Some lines of that budget do, however, merit further discussion here.

I have shown capital income within the income section and then charged it out again (in full) under expenditure. The reason for including it is to have a picture of the total income and the total expenditure of the church. Experience shows that, in years of high capital needs, the normal operating income often suffers. It is wise to be able to see this effect easily and point it out to the church. This is an example of where accounting practices are adapted to meet the needs of the church.

I have shown 'depreciation' under operating expenditure. Depreciation is based on the assumption that capital items lose their value over time, hence some provision should be made for replacing them. It is an accounting concept which actually needs no further cash income and therefore may be unnecessary in a church budget. Most churches will simply make the replacement of any asset the subject of a future decision and appeal. So why have I included it? I have done so, partly because the accounting standards of some countries require it, and partly because it is a real cost even though it has no cash-flow implications. Every church needs to raise cash for capital items, whether replacing the existing items or buying new ones. Using depreciation is one way of ensuring that cash does get raised on a regular basis for such items. You will note that I have also included a capital budget in which this depreciation is simply added to 'capital income', because if the budget is achieved, it will be real cash income and can be spent. The treasurer can also play it safe and use the depreciation from the past year as the income for the current year's capital expenditure. However, this matter of depreciation is an open matter and every treasurer may have his or her own viewpoint.

Faith or foolishness?

All churches must grapple with the matter of how high they should budget. When are they being irresponsible or foolish, and when are they simply demonstrating a lack of faith and attributing it to being 'responsible'? In this and other areas of our Christian work, we are faced with maintaining the balance between two great truths which are incapable of being perfectly reconciled within the human mind: namely the sovereignty of God, on the one hand, and the responsibility of man, on the other. Budgeting is no exception.

Overemphasis on the sovereignty of God can lead to fatalism, apathy and lack of action, trusting that if God so wills, he will provide whatever is needed. Members do little or nothing and then effectively blame God for the results (or lack of them). Intellectually, we claim to be holding to sound doctrine, but in reality we do not expect anything of a sovereign God. We are simply making excuses for our lack of real faith and action, both of which do not go beyond what we can do on our own.

We may also plan *within our perceived current resources* under the pretext of being responsible and claiming that, if God wants something to happen, he will arrange it regardless of our lack of faith. In effect, this limits God to working within our strength, whereas God prefers to work within our *weakness* and to provide beyond our strengths. 'My grace is sufficient for you, for my power is made perfect in weakness' (2 Cor. 12:9). I have always held a secret admiration, even envy, for people who have no resources other than their faith and then go forward in simple trust; God honours them. I have always struggled to leave my money and my personal skills aside when seeking the Lord's will. God does not *need* us to accomplish his purposes! Do not rationalize away your lack of faith.

On the other hand, overemphasis on man's responsibility leads us to believe that we can plan, organize and sell God's work according to the methods of the world. We then claim to be stepping out in faith, but in reality we are stepping up our advertising, manipulation and selling. Churches doing this are often highly successful in raising huge sums of money. They may even spend lavishly and with reckless abandon, all in the name of 'faith'. But is it just another form of foolishness?

The Bible teaches us that, 'Where there is no vision, the people perish' (Prov. 29:18, KJV). A lack of vision must be at least one of the causes of the poor state of much of the evangelical church at present. Too often, I see people who give up *before they have even tried*! The leaders dream, but their vision is not even presented to the church as a challenge *because it may fail* and they will *look* foolish. They shrink from putting their pride on the line. We should budget at the level at which the leadership and the church collectively believe God would have them operate. It may be high, but if this is in the 'discretionary' or 'capital income' area of the budget, it can be responsibly presented with the caveat 'as the Lord provides'. Then, without being disrespectful of God, let him make the decision. Of course, a sovereign God can never truly be impeded, but our lack of faith contradicts his sovereignty. Do we want to do this? Budgets tend to be self-fulfilling prophecies. Budget low, and you get little; budget high, and you get much. At the year's end, and with the benefit of hindsight, the treasurer explains that he did right by budgeting low because little came in! However, no one will ever know what might have happened had the church set a challenging budget coupled with much prayer. In any event, how do you know that God, in his sovereignty, will not send a millionaire with the gift of generosity into your church next week? I know of churches where this has happened. When did your church last pray for such a solution? Do not limit God!

I will illustrate this point from several real experiences:

Case study 1

Many years ago, I was involved with the planting of a new church in the fast-growing eastern suburbs of Pretoria, South Africa. Most of us in the church were under twenty years of age but God was gracious and we also enjoyed the wisdom and experience of a few older folk (they seemed 'old' at the time but were probably only in their forties or fifties!). One attribute of our group was vision, coupled with an unquestioning faith that we would accomplish our vision. This included buying a building plot the day we founded the church and erecting a very adequate building during the next six months. We called our first full-time pastor at the founding meeting, and a second full-time pastor a year later. We also believed in growth by the 'strawberry principle', in which we would plant nearby churches and then encourage them to do the same. Consequently, when a building plot designated for a church came on the market in a neighbouring suburb, we bought it instantly. (I cannot recall where we found the money, but we bought it for cash!) A few years later (and, in fairness, not in line with my view of the timing), the opportunity arose to plant a church based on this plot. One of our pastors at the time was Martin Holdt, an experienced pastor as well as a successful church planter, having started several churches—I will say more about this later.

Soon after the new church got established, it decided to go ahead with a building project which had been designed to be built in stages, but the pastor was eager to build it all at once. The cost of so doing was daunting and probably beyond the 'sensible' estimate of the income potential of the church. But Martin is a man of prayer and faith. He called the church to prayer, including a day of prayer and fasting. One morning, he was called by a lady who said that she could not sleep because she believed that the Lord had laid it on her heart to turn over a substantial investment that was maturing at the time. It paid for around fifteen per cent of the building costs. Then the city council expropriated a portion of the plot for a new intersection they planned on the one corner of the plot. After some haggling, they agreed to pay an amount equivalent to around thirty per cent of the entire building cost. Some forty-five per cent was now covered! The rest came in rapidly. But the story did not end there. The city council later discovered that they did not need the land after all and agreed to lease it back to the church for ninety-nine years at a peppercorn rent (which they never collected); finally, they gave the land back altogether! God's limits are not the aggregate of our resources.

Case study 2

Martin was also involved in the following story:

He had just moved to the bustling mining town of Palaborwa situated in the east of South Africa. Shortly after his arrival, someone from his original home church gave a substantial amount towards the establishment of this new church. Martin mentioned this as a praise item at the next worship service, prompting a suggestion from someone that he should spend it on cement. At that stage, Martin probably did not know much about building, and even less about the keeping qualities of cement, because he did precisely that! The cement was delivered and became a mountain on his front lawn. Then, one morning, the family awoke to the sound of raindrops! Even Martin knew that this was potential trouble, so they grabbed tablecloths, raincoats and anything that might protect the precious cement. But God was faithful again, and soon a man arrived with a tarpaulin, enabling them to save the cement from ruin. Shortly after these events, the government announced a massive cement shortage and Martin discovered that he could sell the commodity at a substantial profit. Of even more value, the builders offered to buy the cement and help Martin build the church when he was ready. The outcome was that a few months later, the church building opened without a mortgage! Was this faith or foolishness? You may form your own view, but I have known Martin for some fifty years and have no doubt about God's provision in these and many more similar stories. However, he never launches out without very considerable prayer. Perhaps that is where so many of our plans go wrong.

Case study 3

Here is a slightly different approach. A church appointed a committee to investigate refurbishing the building. They put a well-founded and sensible challenge to the congregation and very quickly exceeded the target, with members still willing to give more. This indicated that the challenge could have been higher. Encouraged by this success, they then embarked upon a second phase. The lesson is to be sensible, but *not to give up too soon or aim too low.*

It is difficult to know whether the parlous state of the evangelical church at present is due to God withdrawing our lamp or to our own lack of vision and faith coupled with hard work. We are required to be faithful, not just by plodding on in the face of hardship (that certainly), but also by doing our very best in seeking to glorify God. Only after we have tried diligently, prayed much and still failed should we conclude that we may have misread God's purposes.

How do we steer a balance between acknowledging God's sovereignty in a real way and, at the same time, committing ourselves to wise, faithful and diligent service? I am not suggesting foolish faith or irresponsible behaviour. Nor am I suggesting extravagance or the diverting of resources from evangelistic or mission activities into items such as buildings and equipment. Clearly, balance must be maintained between various demands on our resources. But we do have models in church history and, indeed, even in our midst, of God providing for *all* of these needs.

Here is a summary of a possible course of action:

- Pray for the leaders to develop a sensible plan based on a vision for the future which is consistent with the community being served but which is not based on the resources available. (It would be 'foolishness', for example, to plan a mega-church in a desert region of Africa!) It is wrong to add up the incomes of the members and budget a percentage as the likely income of the church. As already pointed out, a millionaire from outside the community could join a month later.
- The leaders (this is one of the main tasks of leadership) must then present this plan to the church (or to some delegated group) for approval. They must persuade the church (another leadership responsibility) to support the plan cheerfully. If it does not, the leaders must re-plan until the church does endorse it cheerfully. Listen to wisdom: 'Without counsel plans fail, but with many

advisers they succeed' (Prov. 15:22). Leaders should submit to God's leading through the body of the church. In this way, we can allow God to reveal his will to us.

- Then pray that the resources will be found to execute the plan. At the same time, keep the needs fresh in the congregation's view. Challenge the members. I am not suggesting that the pastor preaches on giving until all the money has come in—absolutely not. Keep the challenge alive in understated but nevertheless clear ways so that the congregation knows what is still needed. This is simply good leadership and good communication.

- Finally, spend the resources as they come in. This is especially true of capital projects and for the 'discretionary' portions of the operating budget. It could be reckless to spend what the church does not have nor reasonably expects to have. However, I have an open mind on whether or not to borrow to execute a capital plan such as for a building. In some cases, the congregation may see that it is right to borrow because sufficient faith exists that the loan will be repaid. Other congregations may prefer to exercise faith which leads to the cash coming in first. In the final analysis, cash in the bank or loans to be repaid are both expressions of the faith of the congregation. I can, however, see no justification for borrowing to fund the operating budget. This, in my view, would amount to recklessness.

Internal–external balance

Many churches are inwardly focused. By this I mean that they are mainly concerned with keeping themselves going and scarcely finding the time or resources to 'go out' in evangelism (including missions) or make a difference in their community. Churches will generally acknowledge the need to do these things, but sometimes put off doing much 'until they have sorted out some internal problems'. The devil knows this and has a great time keeping the leaders endlessly busy 'sorting out the internal problems'. Strangely, when a church mends its ways and becomes *outwardly focused*, it often finds that the internal problems die down! It is therefore a good health check on a church to analyse the ratio of what is spent on internal items and what is aimed at outwardly focused ministries. This is why, in my model budget, I suggest that you include a column marked '% of total'. Add up the external items and you may be surprised at what it says about your church. I know of a church that, even though small, determined to make this ratio 50:50. Other churches ensure that missionary giving must be at least ten per cent of the total, and so on. There is no right or wrong proportion, but looking at the percentages will reveal the real priorities of the church.

Include the needy

Giving in the New Testament is heavily weighted in favour of giving to the needy. In fact, apart from providing for the pastors and preachers, no mention is made of the administrative and running costs that consume so much of our church budgets. Read Acts 2:44–45: 'And all who believed were together and had all things in common. And they were selling their possessions and belongings and distributing the proceeds to all, as any had need.' Acts 4:32–34 goes on: 'no one said that any of the things that belonged to him was his own, but they had everything in common … There was not a needy person among them, for as many as were owners of lands or houses sold them and brought the proceeds of what was sold.' Paul says, 'For Macedonia and Achaia have been pleased to make some contribution for the poor among the saints at Jerusalem' (Rom. 15:26). And in Galatians 2:10: 'Only, they asked us to remember the poor, the very thing I was eager to do.' Paul's urging in 2 Corinthians 8 is for the needy in Jerusalem. The Old Testament taught the same lesson. Just one verse will suffice: 'Whoever oppresses a poor man insults his Maker, but he who is generous to the needy honours him' (Prov. 14:31). Surely this applies to a church as well?

We could go on. Yet evangelicals have often neglected to follow the precedents of the New Testament church in this regard. Get your church to rethink this item on your budget, beginning with the needs of Christians but extending it to others in need.

Tax

In some countries, donations to a church are either allowed as a deduction from income for tax purposes or, as is the case in the UK, qualify for Gift Aid. Some Christians miss the opportunity of increasing their giving through this mechanism on the grounds that they do not want the government to be funding their churches. A better view of Gift Aid is to see it as a return of some of your taxation—which is what it really is. In the USA, donors are entitled to reduce their taxable incomes by whatever they gave in cash or kind to their church. Other countries have different rules and it should be incumbent on the leaders of a church to investigate what tax relief is available to its congregation. Whatever the mechanism, it is important that the church and the donor alike stay within the law but also maximize the church's income.

In other countries (South Africa is an example), all donations, including those to a church, may attract donations or gift tax unless the church is properly registered and the donations are in accordance with the tax laws governing charities. This means that, unless the church has met certain obligations, the donor may be required to *contribute* tax in addition to the donation to the church. Once again, careful adherence to the tax legislation is called for.

Control

All of us are made in God's image, but all of us are sinners by nature (Rom. 3:23). For this reason, we need to be controlled. Good stewardship of church finances requires three elements of control for every category of expenditure:

- General approval through the budget process, as set out above.
- Specific authorization for someone to approve items within each budget category.
- Reporting of the expenditure back to the leaders and the church.

Every church must work out its own method of doing this. I suggest the following (we are in the realm of freedoms, so I am not being dogmatic):

- Non-discretionary expenditures are wholly delegated to the treasurer to pay without further approvals, though, naturally, he or she must report to the church.
- Discretionary expenditures are delegated to individual elders or deacons. They may spend on individual items up to the amount of the category within the budget, provided that funds are available (i.e. budgeted income is forthcoming). If funds are not available, the treasurer must inform the elder or deacon responsible. Under these circumstances, the elders will have to rule on some priorities. Once again, the elder or deacon (through the treasurer) must report to the church.
- The treasurer will then pay the account once approved by the accountable elder/deacon, or pay the claim when it is submitted.

This method is simple, and it allows elders and deacons to get on with matters within their allocated ministries and within the budget approved by the church. It is efficient and allows all office bearers to avoid committee decisions and to work with or without a team, as appropriate. (Good leadership will still consult, but will not be held up.) The downside is that individual elders or deacons are given considerable authority and not everything they do will please the other elders or deacons, or even, indeed, all the members. Churches will have to decide to take this risk in the interests of moving forward and spending more time and effort spreading the gospel and building up the church than in controlling expenses. Individuals will have to learn the meaning of submission.

What is submission? Let me illustrate. If I say to my wife, 'Here is £100; I will drive you to the nearest shopping mall to spend it', and she comes along because she would love to spend the £100, that is not submission. On the other hand, if I say to her, 'Drive *me* to the nearest shopping mall and I will go shopping while you sit in the car', and she does so, that is submission! (It is also poor behaviour on my part, but that is not the point.) Submission includes accepting that which is *not pleasing to you*, doing what is *not your idea* and, worst of all, doing something that *you do not agree with*. We are called upon to submit to one another (Eph. 5:21) and to submit to our leaders (Heb. 13:17).

Congregational involvement and reports

I have dealt with the role of the congregation in constructing and approving the budget, but two points are worthy of emphasis: being proactive in suggesting or recommending items to be included in the budget; and being given adequate reports on the financial affairs of the church.

Recommendations

No leadership should ever feel so insecure that it does not heed advice from anyone. It is part of the humility required in a servant leader. Moses was one of the greatest leaders of all time, yet note how he was described: 'Now the man Moses was very meek, more than all people who were on the face of the earth' (Num. 12:3). He gladly accepted the advice of his father-in-law Jethro. Allowing members to make recommendations helps the members to feel part of the body, which greatly increases commitment and unity. The leaders should therefore call for budgetary recommendations from the various departments as already described, but also for ideas from any member for items not covered in the usual departmental budgets.

INTERNAL REPORTS

The treasurer must be required to report to the church on a regular basis, ideally once a month to the leaders and perhaps quarterly or even annually to the congregation. It may also be a good idea to give interim reports on the church notice board on a more frequent basis. The simplest report is to use the budget (see the model budget in Appendix 1), adding a column reflecting the latest state of affairs. Any narrative or verbal report should be given in clear, jargon-free terminology. The key issue is to communicate the true state of the church's finances. At all costs, do not make this an accounting exercise!

EXTERNAL REPORTS

In addition to the all-important congregational reports, reports are increasingly required by other bodies. Perhaps your church is within a denomination requiring the filing of annual accounts, or perhaps reports are required by the authorities. It is very important that these reports are presented in accordance with the standards applicable to your country and the recipient of the report. This is just one element of the need to be seen to be doing what is right in the eyes of men (see 2 Cor. 8:18–22) and conforming to the laws of your land; 'Therefore render to Caesar the things that are Caesar's' (Matt. 22:21). Naturally, these external reports should also be circulated within the church, but the internal and external reports should not be confused; they serve different purposes.

Members' responsibilities

Chapter 4

God loves a cheerful giver.

-2 Cor. 9:7

Much of this book is directed at the leadership of a church or at those members who take an active interest in the church's finances. However, the church cannot spend what it does not have, and its money will come mainly from the members and adherents. This chapter is therefore especially relevant to them, or can serve as notes for the leaders to teach the congregation.

When the members vote (or do whatever they do) to approve the church's budget, they are also *committing themselves to giving*. This is nothing new. Long ago, the Israelites were called upon to give to the building and then the running of the tabernacle and temple. It has always cost a lot of money to run and maintain a church as well as meet commitments to the needy. Point out to those who complain that appealing for contributions for the running of a church has a long-standing biblical origin.

We see the Old Testament tithe as a precedent, a demonstration that the congregation was expected, indeed commanded, to contribute at least ten per cent to the running of the tabernacle and then the temple. The word 'tithe' occurs in seventeen verses of the Old Testament in the English Standard Version. However, the people actually gave more than the tithe because they gave 'freewill offerings' as well. The Old Testament provides many examples of how this worked. Consider just a few verses as illustrations:

- 'To the Levites I have given every tithe in Israel for an inheritance, in return for their service that they do, *their service in the tent of meeting*' (Num. 18:21, emphasis added).
- 'And he commanded the people who lived in Jerusalem

to give the portion due to the priests and the Levites, that they might give themselves to the Law of the LORD. As soon as the command was spread abroad, the people of Israel gave in abundance the firstfruits of grain, wine, oil, honey, and of all the produce of the field. And they brought in abundantly the tithe of everything' (2 Chr. 31:4–5).

- 'For the people of Israel and the sons of Levi shall bring the contribution of grain, wine, and oil to the chambers, where the vessels of the sanctuary are, as well as the priests who minister, and the gatekeepers and the singers. *We will not neglect the house of our God*' (Neh. 10:39, emphasis added).

If the people under the law of the Old Testament gave a tithe and more, how much more should we give out of love for a Saviour who died for us? He 'bought' us at a price.

Much of what I have said about budgeting is in the realm of freedom and the quotations from the Old Testament show precedents. We will now look at some New Testament principles which should govern our giving to the work of the Lord.

It is worthwhile looking again in detail at what Paul wrote to the Corinthians (citing the giving of the Macedonians) in 2 Corinthians 8:1–16 (verse numbers have been included for ease of reference):

[1]We want you to know, brothers, about the grace of God that has been given among the churches of Macedonia, [2]for in a severe test of affliction, their abundance of joy and their extreme poverty have overflowed in a wealth of generosity on their part. [3]For they gave according to their means, as I can testify, and beyond their means, of their own free will, [4]begging us earnestly for the favour of taking part in the relief of the saints—[5]and this, not as we expected, but they gave themselves first to the

Lord and then by the will of God to us. [6]Accordingly, we urged Titus that as he had started, so he should complete among you this act of grace. [7]But as you excel in everything—in faith, in speech, in knowledge, in all earnestness, and in our love for you—see that you excel in this act of grace also. [8]I say this not as a command, but to prove by the earnestness of others that your love also is genuine. [9]For you know the grace of our Lord Jesus Christ, that though he was rich, yet for your sake he became poor, so that you by his poverty might become rich. [10]And in this matter I give my judgement: this benefits you, who a year ago started not only to do this work but also to desire to do it. [11]So now finish doing it as well, so that your readiness in desiring it may be matched by your completing it out of what you have. [12]For if the readiness is there, it is acceptable according to what a person has, not according to what he does not have. [13]I do not mean that others should be eased and you burdened, but that as a matter of fairness [14]your abundance at the present time should supply their need, so that their abundance may supply your need, that there may be fairness. [15]As it is written, 'Whoever gathered much had nothing left over, and whoever gathered little had no lack.' [16]But thanks be to God, who put into the heart of Titus the same earnest care I have for you.

Here are some of the lessons about giving from this passage:

They first gave themselves to God and then to man (v. 5)

This is always the priority. We make sure of our vertical relationship with God and then implement the second great commandment, namely to love our neighbours, through giving.

Giving was an act of grace (vv. 1, 6–7)

Giving was generous even though the givers were poor:

'... their extreme poverty [has] overflowed in a wealth of generosity' (v. 2). We will expand on this point later.

Giving was out of their 'own free will' (v. 3)

Giving was voluntary and proportional to their ability—and beyond it. Could it have been a tithe? It may well have been more (v. 2).

They gave out of a heart of love, i.e. real concern for others (v. 8)

Admittedly, this is referring to giving for famine relief. However, the principles remain the same for all giving to the church. In addition, every church should include 'goodwill' or poverty alleviation in its budget.

Now to elaborate on these principles:

Giving is not a matter of compulsion nor of commandment

Note that when Ananias and Sapphira sold their land and gave some of the proceeds to the apostles, they were told, 'While it remained unsold, did it not remain your own? And after it was sold, was it not *at your disposal*?' (Acts 5:4, emphasis added). They were free to give or not to give. Their deaths were caused not because they hadn't given everything but because they had lied to the Holy Spirit.

Giving follows our priorities

If entertainment, travel, sport, clothing or food (all legitimate 'things') are at the centre of our lives, then the Lord's work will get the leftovers. Listen to John's blunt warning:

> Do not love the world or the things in the world. If anyone loves the world, the love of the Father is not in him. For all that is in the world— the *desires of the flesh*

and the desires of the eyes and pride in possessions—is not from the Father but is from the world. And the world is *passing away* along with its desires, but whoever does the will of God abides for ever.

1 John 2:15–17, emphasis added

Giving should be voluntary and cheerful

'Each one must give as he has made up his mind, not reluctantly or under compulsion, for God loves a cheerful giver' (2 Cor. 9:7). We also read, '… they gave … of their *own free will*' (8:3, emphasis added).

Giving should be proportional to our wealth

'Now concerning the collection for the saints … On the first day of every week, each of you is to put something aside and store it up, as he may prosper' (1 Cor. 16:1–2). The term 'as he may prosper' is translated 'according to his financial ability' in some versions, which perhaps better conveys its meaning to us. This rendering is in line with 2 Corinthians 8:3: 'they gave according to their means'.

Giving should be sacrificial

And he sat down opposite the treasury and watched the people putting money into the offering box. Many rich people put in large sums. And a poor widow came and put in two small copper coins, which make a penny. And he called his disciples to him and said to them, 'Truly, I say to you, this poor widow has put in more than all those who are contributing to the offering box. For they all contributed out of their abundance, but she out of her poverty has put in everything she had, all she had to live on.'

Mark 12:41–44

This strictly is a precedent, but note that Jesus called his disciples and *taught* them from this precedent. Dare *we* ignore the lesson? Jesus was teaching here that giving is part of our worship. It is a demonstration of our love for him and of our priorities. God does not need our 'giving' to build the church. He can do anything without our help. We must therefore stop thinking of giving solely to meet a need or a challenge (although it certainly may include that) but primarily as an act of worship.

Giving should be generous

The Old Testament set a precedent for us in specifying the tithe (i.e. ten per cent), but even within the legalism of the Old Testament, people gave freewill offerings in addition to the tithe. Some writers believe that the tithe continues into our age, but that it should be given out of gratitude, not legalism. Consider Jesus' words: 'Woe to you, scribes and Pharisees, hypocrites! For you tithe mint and dill and cumin … These you ought to have done' (Matt. 23:23). Is Jesus saying that we all ought to tithe, or is he merely saying this to the legalists who hoped by good works to find a way to heaven? I am not sure, but I find it difficult to produce a convincing proof for tithing as a principle. Another reason why I will not push the point is that surely we should give much more. I see the tithe as a precedent for a good *starting point*. The early church set an even more impressive precedent by sometimes giving *all* of the proceeds from the sale of properties: 'There was not a needy person among them, for as many as were owners of lands or houses sold them and *brought the proceeds* of what was sold' (Acts 4:34, emphasis added). This was no tithe! I am not suggesting that we all *must* do this—it may be poor stewardship—but I am suggesting that we should follow their lead and *be generous*. Paul said this directly in his instructions to the rich: 'They are to do good, to be rich in good works, to be *generous* and ready to share' (1 Tim. 6:18, emphasis added).

Finally, listen to Paul's clear urging:

The point is this: whoever sows sparingly will also reap sparingly, and whoever sows bountifully will also reap bountifully. Each one must give as he has made up his mind, not reluctantly or under compulsion, for God loves a cheerful giver. And God is able to make all grace abound to you, so that having all sufficiency in all things at all times, you may abound in every good work.

2 Cor. 9:6–8

Limitations

Are there any limitations on what church members may or may not do with their giving? Yes, they may not *manipulate* the leadership. Let me explain this by way of two illustrations:

Case study 1

When I was a teenager, I became concerned about my pastor's car. It was old, dilapidated and unreliable. He did not mind any of this as his priorities were elsewhere, but it grieved me (and many other members), so I decided to do something about it. Nothing wrong so far. I *assumed* that the church could not afford to give him a new one and that the leaders were doing nothing about it. (I have never determined whether or not these assumptions were justified.) Consequently, I proceeded to find a way of getting him a new car at a discount and to raise the cash to buy it. I then presented the leaders with something approaching a done deal. No one doubted my motives, and the church was grateful for the income and the arrangements to get the car cheaply. But the leaders were angry with me on two counts: firstly, I had shown them up; and secondly, I had manipulated them into doing what *they* had not decided to do. I was naively surprised at their reaction but, looking back, they were right. It was not for me to show them up in this way

55

(maybe they *were* doing something about the problem); and I had robbed them of *their* responsibility to decide on how best to spend the finances of the church.

What should I have done? There must never be any reluctance from anybody to make recommendations to the church leaders. Nor should there be any resentment by leaders at hearing suggestions and accepting income raised by an enthusiastic member. It is entirely possible that my church leaders would have reacted correctly had I allowed them to do so. I should have politely (is this possible for a teenager with a mission?) made some suggestions and offered my assistance. Then I should have submitted to *whatever* they decided. *They* were accountable and would have to answer to God for the pastor's safety and convenience. I should also have accepted that, once I had given any funds to the leaders, the cash *belonged to the church*. The leaders then had both the privilege and the responsibility to spend it on whatever they considered to be the highest priority in the church. It may not have been on a new car; perhaps they would have bought a used one and given some of the money to missions. Yet I didn't allow them to exercise their God-given responsibilities.

Cast study 2

At another time, a visitor began attending my church. He was wealthy and generous, and my church was young and short of many resources. This visitor soon noticed that we had no organ but sang to a piano. One Sunday, however, we discovered a high-quality electronic organ at the front of the church, obviously donated by him. Everyone was grateful to this new friend and appreciated both his generosity and his excellent spirit. But was he right in doing this? I do not question his motives nor his love for both God and the church. However, it is doubtful that the elders had an organ on their priority lists. We were entering a phase when other instruments were becoming more popular in worship and, moreover, the church had many other needs and would no doubt have spent any donated money in other ways. The leadership and the church's more pressing needs were basically ignored. When my wife and I visited the church many years later we noticed that the organ was still in its place but under a neat cover.

Members of a church's congregation should also not simply buy something that they judge the church to need and then say that this is their 'giving' to the Lord's work. Only if the item has been approved by the church or the leadership is it in order for members to respond with a restricted (or specified) donation. But often we are tempted to buy things that are more in line with satisfying *our needs* than the needs of the church. Check yourself!

Members may 'earmark' or 'specify' donations to causes which the church *has already named as needs*, but they should avoid deciding on their own what these needs might be. I know that this can be very frustrating and, on occasions, I have been bursting to drop a cheque in the offering marked for this or that rather obvious need. But it is wrong to bypass the leadership; *it is an act of non-submission*, which is a sin. May we all learn the virtue of submitting to our leaders and to one another (Heb. 13:17; Eph. 5:21).

Reluctant giving

I am concerned by the poor financial state of many evangelical causes which is due to poor giving by Christians. This is less true of the USA than elsewhere, but even in the USA it is reported that church giving only amounts to a mere two per cent of the income of its members. Why is this so when, in general, Christians in the West are relatively so well off?

I suspect that, instead of giving in accordance with the principles set out above, we give from our spare cash with, maybe, just a little sacrifice. I notice how readily we all spend on our pleasures. How easily we spend quite large sums on theatre or sports tickets, restaurant dinners and parties, but put comparatively small sums into the offering on Sunday! Expensive holidays, often abroad, have become 'our right'. Keeping up with the latest fashions has become a high priority. I am not suggesting that God does not intend us to enjoy all that he has graciously given us, but are we considering Jesus' command to 'seek first the kingdom of God and his righteousness and all these things will be added to you' (Matt. 6:33)? This command is given in the context of our practical, material needs (vv. 25–33). It is worth pausing here for a moment to consider what constitutes the 'needs' that Jesus says our heavenly Father will provide. When Jesus made this promise, 'needs' would have been simple and probably covered little more than food and clothing (he actually mentions these items in v. 31, so we can be absolutely sure about these); they would also have included housing and transport. Joseph, Jesus' father, appears to have owned a donkey, and Peter and John had boats. The disciples in Acts owned 'lands or houses' (Acts 4:34). We should, however, recognize that, over the years, living standards in the West have improved hugely so that one-time luxuries have now become 'needs'. God knows this because he has graciously given us the 'enabling' technologies that have made improvements in living standards possible. Furthermore, he gave mankind the garden of Eden, 'where there is gold', to 'subdue'. (Gen. 2:11; 1:28). Why mention gold if it was not intended to be used to develop an economy in which everyone could enjoy all the good things that God intended for his children? God does not deny us all the blessings (including material ones) that he intended for us;

it is sin which keeps us from enjoying his blessings. The central issue is not, therefore, how great a proportion of our modern living standards we may regard as 'needs', but rather whether or not we 'seek *first* the kingdom of God'—in other words, this is about our priorities. My own experience has been that, when I endeavour to seek him first, God has blessed me beyond my dreams in *all things material, but this is not always going to be the case.*

We should take seriously these further words of Jesus: 'Do not lay up for yourselves treasures on earth, where moth and rust destroy and where thieves break in and steal, but lay up for yourselves treasures in heaven, where neither moth nor rust destroys and where thieves do not break in and steal' (Matt. 6:19–20). In the UK banking crisis of 2007/8, my wife and I became very aware of the insecurity of our bank balances. We had invested, as we thought, in an ultra-conservative manner by putting our money into a number of banks, avoiding any high-risk stock-market-linked investments. Then those very banks teetered! God spoke to us through this period and we changed our priorities, moving substantial sums into the Lord's work, where 'neither moth nor rust destroys and where thieves do not break in and steal'. The 'thieves' in that crisis were all those who had gone beyond normal borrowing and lending and had been driven by greed.

One pastor tells a story of a lady who was left by her husband to fend for herself and her family. With sadness, she told the pastor that, by the end of each month, she had little left for the Lord's work. He suggested that she should decide what she intended to give and then give it *cheerfully* at the *commencement* of each month. Later, she reported how much easier it had become to make ends meet now that she gave to the Lord's work *first*. The Bible teaches, 'Therefore the LORD the God of Israel declares: "... for those who honour me I will honour, and those who despise me shall be lightly esteemed"' (1 Sam. 2:30). This lady had learnt to prioritize her giving, and it was met with blessing from God.

All Christians should periodically reconsider how they allocate their money. 'And Jesus, looking at him, loved him, and said to him, "You lack one thing: go, sell all that you have and give to the poor, and you will have treasure in heaven; and come, follow me"' (Mark 10:21).

Specified giving

What about giving to causes other than the local church?

My view is that we are called upon to 'Bring the full tithes into the storehouse …' (Mal. 3:10). I do not think that we can make a principle of this in the New Testament church, but I do think that we can develop some useful 'freedoms' from this verse:

- We should aim to bring in *all* the tithes to the storehouse, which I see as the local church today.
- This implies that, even when we wish to give to a para-church organization, we should do it through our local church. Your gift should be clearly marked and the treasurer should keep a record of all such channelled giving together with suitable reports so that all can see which ministries are being supported by various members.
- A valuable side effect of this approach is that it gives the leadership a measure of the real total giving capacity of the church.
- Such 'specified' or 'restricted' donations must be carefully handled for tax purposes. In the UK, for example, such donations will only qualify for Gift Aid if the final recipient is also entitled to Gift Aid (in which case the Gift Aid should be passed on as well), or if the recipient is in an activity which falls within the normal scope of the activities of the church. This

latter condition is also necessary for the donation not to attract donations tax in South Africa. In other tax jurisdictions, expert advice should be sought.

- A possible objection to this approach is that it 'manipulates' the church into supporting a particular ministry which the leaders may not otherwise have supported. This is true, but at least it indicates to the leaders which ministries the members are supporting and allows them to take whatever action they deem fit. Another objection is that it can complicate the work of the treasurer, involving him or her in a lot of 'post office' work. One way around this is for the donor to send the money directly but inform the treasurer, thereby at least giving the leaders an idea of which organizations members are supporting and a measure of the giving capacity.

Pastors' and paid workers' remuneration

For the Scripture says, 'You shall not muzzle an ox when it treads out the grain', and, 'The labourer deserves his wages.'

–1 Tim. 5:18

There is a poor joke that says that pastors should be humble, and that it is the duty of the church to assist them in this noble aim by keeping them poor. Nothing could be further from the truth—that is, about keeping the pastor poor! The Bible is *not silent* on how we should pay our pastors and, by extension, other workers in the church. We will look at some biblical precedents and then some principles, followed by some ideas in the realm of freedom which will help us achieve the biblical principles.

Precedents occur in the Old Testament, even down to protecting the rights of animals. They were to be paid (i.e. fed) as they worked: 'You shall not muzzle an ox when it is treading out the grain' (Deut. 25:4). Paul quotes this verse to make it clear that it also refers to paying the labourer, not so much the ox: 'For it is written in the Law of Moses, "You shall not muzzle an ox when it treads out the grain." Is it for oxen that God is concerned?' (1 Cor. 9:9). Clearly the answer is 'no'. Elsewhere, after quoting the same verse, he adds, '"The labourer deserves his wages"' (1 Tim. 5:18), placing it in the context of paying an elder. In 1 Corinthians 9:13–14, he says, 'Do you not know that those who are employed in the temple service get their food from the temple, and those who serve at the altar share in the sacrificial offerings? In the same way, the Lord commanded that those *who proclaim the gospel should get their living by the gospel*' (emphasis added).

Paul is building on the precedent of the tithe received by the Levite priests in the temple (see Num. 18:21). This enabled them to work in the 'house of the Lord' without the need to do other work.

We now turn to some principles from the New Testament.

The New Testament leaves us in no doubt about the principle that churches should pay those who work as elders or pastors, and pay them well. 'Let the elders who rule well be considered worthy of double honour, especially those who labour in preaching and teaching' (1 Tim. 5:17). Paul goes on to quote the Old Testament verse referred to above about the labourer being worthy of his hire. He therefore clearly has pay on his mind. Note that he applies this special consideration to the elders who rule and especially those 'who labour in preaching and teaching', that is, the person we tend to call the 'pastor'. What is the meaning of the term 'double honour'? Some versions translate this expression as 'double stipend'. Does this mean double pay? Double whose pay? I am not sure that we need to solve this translation issue to the last per cent, but what *is* clear is that pastors should not be badly paid! Yet we must admit that some churches do pay their pastor badly. This is wrong. We should err on the side of generosity. I will deal with some specific ideas later when we consider our freedoms in this matter.

Paul reinforces this position in a detailed argument in 1 Corinthians 9:1–14, summing it all up with this verse: 'In the same way, the Lord commanded that those who proclaim the gospel should get their living by the gospel' (1 Cor. 9:14); Paul goes on to say that he did not make use of this right. He was making sure that the church understood that it was *obliged* to pay its workers. The church must accept its responsibilities and be prepared to pay anyone who works for it. On the other hand, the pastor (and other workers) may decline any portion or the entire wage offered. They should not be embarrassed if they accept what is on offer in its entirety.[4]

Another principle that Paul presents is that, when men travel in the cause of the gospel, they are entitled to take their wives along with them. Note Paul's rhetorical question: 'Do we not have the right to take along a believing wife, as do the other apostles and the brothers of the Lord and Cephas?' (1 Cor. 9:5; Paul himself cites a precedent here). We can easily guess Paul's reason for teaching this way. He is being consistent with his teaching that the best way to avoid moral failure is for a man to have his wife with him at all times (1 Cor. 7:9). In times when journeys were of long duration, it was no good being separated from your wife for long periods. But is this principle of no value today? I suggest that wives should endeavour to travel with their husbands whenever they are away from home for any reasonable length of time, and that churches should face up to this expense.

We now move into some practical ideas which are all in the realm of freedom but which satisfy the principles taught in the Bible. Clearly, these issues may be resolved for many churches in that the employment contract between the church and its employees may be determined by the denomination. Even in these circumstances, it may be useful to study the remainder of this chapter as well as Appendix 2 in order to check the adequacy of the existing contract.

The most pressing issue is how much to pay the pastor. I have already argued that we should err on the side of generosity (double honour), but we need some benchmark. A good starting point is to consider the typical member of the church. If the church is in Beverly Hills and every member is a millionaire, the church should determine what a typical (not average) member would earn and target a similar salary for the pastor. After all, his costs will also be high. If, on the other hand, the church is in Africa and the typical member is a subsistence farmer, then the pastor should be given sufficient to subsist alongside his brethren. If a church is in an affluent suburb of New York, London, Johannesburg or Sydney, the typical members may well be stockbrokers! In these churches, a salary pitched at their level would be appropriate. For most of us, however, the church will be in middle-class suburbia. For these churches, a typical member will be a school teacher or other professional. I note with interest (and approval) that in the UK, the Fellowship of Independent Evangelical Churches (FIEC) publishes the UK teacher's pay scales and recommends that these be used as benchmarks. It is possible to use these scales to determine where your church fits in because they are given in terms of seniority scales and years of experience, and include adjustments for inflation. If your church membership includes a substantial number of professional and business people, you may want to use the scales for head teachers or even professors. The basic principle is that, in financial terms, the pastor should not be seriously out of line with his church membership. As I said earlier, if he is happy to take less, he should be allowed to do so, but the church must act honourably.

The next issue is to determine the salaries of other pastors and workers who may be employed by the church. All should be treated in accordance with the same principles given above. The only exception mentioned in the Bible is the case we have already noted: that the elder who rules, teaches and preaches, that is, the (lead?) pastor, is worthy of double honour. This can be used as a check at the end to see whether that elder does end up with a total package that is roughly double that of other workers. In the scheme I suggest below, it will come close!

Before we go any further, let me clarify which workers we are considering. I am not suggesting that everyone who does anything for the church should be paid. Many people who work 'after hours' and have other paid employment should not be included unless their income is less than that which the church would have paid if *they were in the full-time employ of the church*. In such a case, the church *may* pay those workers something to 'top up' their incomes. In general, therefore, I am referring to people who work for the church on a regular basis and thereby curtail their opportunity to earn a living elsewhere. If they work part-time, they should be paid by applying the policy to a full-time position in the church and then paying a pro rata portion. Alternatively, they can be paid an hourly rate based on a similar secular job. If they work partly in the church and partly elsewhere, the church should calculate what it would have paid and then deduct the portion that the outside employer pays. This is all set out in the model policy in Appendix 2.

In my experience, pastors may fall into one of two equally wrong traps. Pastors should check their activities, but churches also have a duty to guard their pastors from falling into these traps.

The first trap is that pastors devote themselves to their jobs almost to the exclusion of everything else. The consequences are often dysfunctional families and broken health. My wife and I had the great privilege of growing up under a pastor whose commitment was well beyond anything reasonable. I say 'privilege' because he was a huge gift to the church and one of the godliest men I have ever known. But he burnt himself out for the church and it is only by God's grace that all of his children have turned out well (one is himself a fine pastor). His health collapsed at a relatively early age and he spent his last years in a mental home. I still feel humbled when I think about him and I shrink from criticizing him. But I would fail all pastors who read this book if I did not warn them not to emulate this model. Church leaders should insist that their pastor takes a day off each week, goes away on vacation and maintains the correct work–recreation–family balance. Pastors should not resent their colleagues intruding into their private lives in this way.

The second extreme is the pastor who lacks personal drive and self-discipline and is seen as a 'shirker' (I refrain from stronger language!). He may put in the same hours as secular workers but they may be of little value because they lack focus and drive. The pastorate offers ample opportunity to be a shirker, even if unintentionally; at least, it offers the opportunity to be *perceived* as such. The principle of transparency teaches that the pastor should ensure that he *does* work hard and that this is *known* to his congregation. If not, it may diminish the value of his ministry. A serious and experienced church member once told me that his church paid for a full-time pastor but got a part-time one! I did not agree, but I could understand how he had come to this conclusion. Pastors are often paid less than they deserve because of a perception that they do not work hard enough to justify a decent salary. I know that it takes a lot of reading and hard work to prepare a good sermon, but it is possible to become a 'bookworm', reading well beyond what is needed. It is also possible to read slowly and dream along the way. None of this is efficient use of time. Pastors claiming this approach must ensure that their sermons reflect the many hours of reading and preparation. I know of a family who belonged to a church which enjoyed the ministry of a fine pastor. However, they were so incensed when the church proposed giving the pastor a modest pay increase that they resigned their membership! Clearly, these situations must be avoided so that the devil gets no foothold in sowing discontent in the church. Church leaders should coach pastors who lack the skills and drive to work effectively and *efficiently*. The pastor in this situation should not resent his colleagues assisting him in planning his activities.

In all cases, the church leaders must inform the congregation of the pastor's activities so that the principle of transparency is maintained. Some simple examples include giving details of any absence from the normal meetings of the church, giving the church advance notice of vacation leave or outside preaching engagements and so on. I remember visiting a church where it was announced that the pastor would not be present at the evening service because he was joining his family, who were playing in a musical concert. While I refrain from commenting on the reason for his absence, I give full marks for giving this information openly and clearly. What did amaze me was the real resentment of some members of his family, who objected to him telling the church. They could not understand why the church had to be told about family arrangements. My wife pointed out that the church paid the pastor's salary and normally expected him to be working on a Sunday.

I strongly recommend that pastors study *On Being a Pastor* by Derek Prime and Alistair Begg,[5] which deals with the issues that I raise above.

We now need to reflect on the different theories of remuneration. Purist communism teaches that everyone should be paid what he or she *needs* regardless of what he or she contributes. Purist capitalism teaches that everyone should be paid in accordance with what he or she *contributes*, regardless of what he or she needs. As always, Christians are not obliged to fit into any man-made categorization. Remember how Jesus taught that the worker who did one hour could be paid the same as the workers who had toiled all day? Modern remuneration theorists would be horrified! Jesus did this because he cared for the workers who *needed* a full day's wages to live and was showing compassion on the late-comers; in other words, pay was according to their *need*. Jesus also taught that workers could be rewarded for 'good and faithful service', that is, in relation to their *contribution*. I suggest that Christians are free to do a little of each. Consequently, the policy guide in Appendix 2 assumes a combination of *contribution* and *need*.

Case study

I know of a pastor in the USA who works from home. Every day, he goes to his study, closes the door and either works there from 8am to 5pm or is involved with church work elsewhere. He declines any family-related activities during that time because his view is that the average father in his congregation is at work during those hours and is subject to the same discipline. He also does not include midweek meetings or attendance at committee meetings as part of his paid work. He teaches that all church members are expected to attend these meetings in their unpaid time, so he does the same. The key issue is that, if pastors are paid properly and in line with a typical member of their churches, they must accept the same responsibilities as well.

I will now explain in more detail some of the elements set out in the suggested policy guide.

Before dealing with the practical details of this issue, readers should refresh their knowledge of the principles governing pastor's salaries as set out above, because in this section we are in the arena of freedoms which must be kept within those principles.

Firstly, to deal effectively with this all-important and emotive issue, I suggest that a 'remuneration committee' be appointed by the church. It should comprise at least one elder, the treasurer and at least one deacon, preferably none of whom should be an employee of the church. It may even include a member who is skilled in these matters and is trusted by the members. Details of the package or packages thus determined may be kept confidential to the extent permitted by law, but the final package 'cost to the church' of all remuneration must be reflected in the 'Salaries' line of the budget for church approval. This automatically gives approval to the details as well.

Salary

I have already suggested to readers in the UK that they use the FIEC guidelines. Naturally, readers in other countries can access these as well and make the necessary currency and cost-of-living adjustments. Alternatively, they can obtain similar information for their own countries.

If, however, a church wishes to 'go it alone' and develop a structure which combines both need and contribution, then the salary section of the policy guide set out in Appendix 2 will help.

This policy begins with a 'basic salary' that would be paid to a young man directly out of training, unmarried and with no experience. His salary should line up with whichever benchmark we have chosen, perhaps that of a young school teacher also just out of college. Other workers in the church can then receive a proportionally lower basic salary. I suggest the following reductions: 85% for an associate pastor; 72% for a junior pastor; 60% for a secretary, and so on; but these percentages should be determined by the remuneration committee and then held constant. The purpose of applying the same *policy* but with different factors to all paid workers in the church is to reduce the potential for human jealousy which so often arises in these situations. Remember Jesus' parable of the workers who arrived at different hours of the day but were all paid the same wage? This appeared to the workers to be 'unfair', a normal human reaction. Jesus taught that we should not think this way, but the fact remains that we are all human and suffer from the same weakness. Most of us will try to figure out why an assistant pastor with a wife and six children earns more than the lead pastor whose children have all left home. The policy set out here endeavours to explain this, based on an attempt to be logical and consistent. It is better than having arbitrary numbers developed at different times for different workers, which is what sometimes happens in churches.

To this basic salary, then, we add amounts which should reflect 'needs' (we are now following communist ideology!). These are for a wife and then children. I suggest 30% for the wife (limited to one!) and 15% for each child (perhaps limited to the size of a typical church member's family, or else the congregation may begin to resent the arrival of each new baby!).

We then endeavour to reward contribution. Clearly, this is difficult, and some judgement may be needed in addition to the mechanical method suggested. Never forget the examples from church history of men such as Spurgeon, who made a huge contribution from nineteen years of age and without the benefit of a college degree! Clearly, my suggestions would not have worked for him. Bear in mind, too, that we are firmly in the freedoms arena and nothing that I say should be regarded as more than a guide. In general, however, contribution should improve with experience and qualifications. The remuneration committee can always add a further factor for outstanding contribution.

Next come 'fringe benefits'. Many of these are not really 'benefits' at all because they may be necessities in doing the job. A car allowance is an obvious example as it may (but not necessarily) be required for a pastor to do his job. Other fringe benefits may be valid only in the context of tax legislation. This calls for someone with tax knowledge to structure the package correctly. Let me illustrate the problem with an example from the church where I was once the treasurer. We intended providing a home (manse) for our pastor and decided to do this by renting an apartment. We were not sure how to structure this from a tax perspective, so visited our tax office to make sure that we were being sensible. To our surprise, we found that it all depended on *how* we paid the rent. If we handed the cheque to the pastor each month and he paid it to the landlord, the rent was simply added to the pastor's income and would be taxed at the full rate. But if we posted the cheque directly to the owner and then made the apartment available to the pastor as a manse, he was taxed at a small flat rate applicable to all manses! Check each item carefully, because some may be taxed and others not, depending on the tax regime under which your church operates. Taxes are often a function on what you call allowances and how you structure them.

Some churches do not employ a full-time pastor and instead use visiting preachers. All of the principles set out above still apply, notably that 'those *who proclaim the gospel should get their living by the gospel*' and that 'the worker deserves his wages'. Churches should note that a preacher does not merely work for the hour or so that he leads the worship and preaches, but typically spends several hours in preparation as well. Moreover, he will travel to and from the place of worship, which may also take several hours. In summary, the church should pay him about one full day's salary—in other words, about three per cent of a full-time pastor's monthly salary—plus travel at whatever rate the tax authorities allow.

Housing

The matter of a manse or church-provided home is a major item and worthy of some serious consideration.

I prefer a scheme in which the church assists the pastor to acquire his own house rather than providing him with a church-owned manse. The advantages of doing this are as follows:

- The capital gains made in the house should accrue to the pastor and not to the church. Churches are generally pleased to see their assets grow, but the church should remind itself that growing assets is never within any church's mission. Pastors often receive meagre pensions and have no home of their own when they do 'go on pension' (I refrain from referring to 'retirement' as I do not see this as a biblical option). If, on the other hand, they do own a home of their own, they can either live in it or sell it and move to wherever they decide to spend their closing years.

- Pastors do well to be faced with the same realities of home ownership as are their members. It is good for them to face varying mortgage payments and to understand the pressure of a broken boiler or an overgrown lawn! It also allows a true comparison to be made of the total income of the pastor on the same basis as that of the typical member. Most members have to rent or buy their own homes.

- When a pastor owns his own home, he signals his intent

to put down roots and stay. 'Once-off' frustrations are more likely to be tolerated and worked through. Research shows that long-serving pastors achieve more than those pastors who move on as soon as they or their congregations learn of each other's human shortcomings.

Some pastors, however, will not want to accept these responsibilities. I recall working hard to convince a new pastor to our church of the benefits to both him and the church. He reluctantly agreed. Then, many years later, I was speaking at a pastor's conference and, after proposing this solution, the once-reluctant pastor was first on his feet to support the scheme proposed here. He had found it a great blessing. As that pastor approaches pension, I am sure he will find it a double blessing.

Loans

Churches must be realistic about how much capital will be needed by a pastor to get started in a scheme in which the pastor buys his own home, car and so on. But if they are converting from an existing arrangement in which the church already owns the property, the church can easily loan the pastor the necessary deposit when it sells the manse to him. Another way around the problem of capital is to enter into an equity partnership in which the house is jointly owned by the church and the pastor. I know that such schemes are fairly common in the UK and the FIEC office can advise churches on implementing them. Other countries will, no doubt, have worked out similar schemes. It is essential that the details of the arrangements are concluded in strict accordance with the law because, among other things, this is a 'related-party transaction'.

The same capital problem arises if the church requires the pastor to own his own car and pays him an allowance when he uses the car on church business. Once again, the church may need to loan the pastor cash. If the church happens to have cash available, it should loan as much as possible to the pastor, as it is poor stewardship to buy a car using high-interest credit. (This is true for the members as well, but beyond the scope of this book. I refer readers to works by Larry Burkett on household financial stewardship.[6]) The model policy in Appendix 2 allows for loans up to double the pastor's annual salary.

Time off

Another source of possible discontent in churches is the time that a pastor takes off for leave, conferences or preaching elsewhere. Some churches take a liberal view and encourage the pastor to travel and widen his ministry. They see the world as their ministry and also believe that the pastor gains fresh vision by visiting other places and churches. Many of us will have benefited from the ministry of 'big name' preachers and teachers who have been allowed by their home churches to travel to conferences or on preaching tours. However, the members of those home churches may not feel too happy about the loss of their valued pastors. It is vital, therefore, that a policy is clearly defined by the leaders and, as in all things, that the congregation should be 'pleased' with the outcome (remember Acts 6:5). Once again, the model policy offers some suggestions in this regard. It suggests various forms of leave, including one ('official leave') which is not deducted from the pastor's normal vacation leave and which allows him to practise a wider ministry.

Review

Finally, the remuneration committee should meet every year to update the package for inflation and other relevant changes. But rapid changes to the scheme or the relative values of allowances and so on should be made with care, as they may undermine fairness and adequacy.

Conclusion

Churches which claim to be founded on the Bible must endeavour to be biblical in all they do. They cannot present a challenge to their members to follow the Bible in their private lives, their relationships, their work and recreation, yet fail to implement the same meticulous attention to detail in the running of the church. Such action would be hypocrisy. This principle applies to the finances of the church as much as to all other organizational aspects. Furthermore, the allocations within the budget are an outward expression of the church's priorities. The manner in which funds are collected and spent is a manifestation of how seriously biblical principles are applied in practical matters.

Members must also re-evaluate their priorities in order to determine what they give to the church and other ministries.

APPENDIX 1. EXAMPLE OF CHURCH BUDGET AND REPORT

Model church budget

Description	Last year actual	This year forecast	Next year budget	% of total	Year to date actual	Use this column for comments on budget and later for comments on actuals
Income						
Offerings						What is placed in the 'plate' each week
Donations						Only if required as a separate item
Specified (restricted income)						Such as missions, youth, etc.
Sale of books, CDs, DVDs, refreshments, etc.						Essentially money recovered for items
Gift aid (UK only)						Or any other form of external income
Interest						Assumes that the church holds surplus cash, otherwise zero
Surplus carried forward from last year						If income exceeded expenditure
Capital income						Specified for capital projects
Gross income to church						This yields the cash income level of the church for all funds

Expenditure								
Non-discretionary expenditure								*Definition will vary from church to church*
Salaries—total expenditure								*Include that of pastor and any paid workers*
Property taxes								
Utilities								
Vehicles								*Church buses, pastor's vehicle, etc.*
Telephones								*Pastor's and any church telephone*
Building maintenance and cleaning								
Insurance								
Office expenses								
Depreciation of assets								*This is optional—see Chapter 3 for discussion*
Over-expenditure carried forward from last year								*Only if expenditure exceeded income*
Total non-discretionary expenditure								

Discretionary expenditure (cash flow)						
Missions						These items will vary from church to church and must follow the overall vision of the church
Outreach/promotion/evangelism events						
Music						
Various ministries, e.g. missions, youth, men's						
Refreshments						
Printing, stationery and postage						
Books, CDs and DVDs						
Goodwill (benevolent or social concern)						Money given to those in need
Conferences and travel						
Expenditure						
Non-discretionary expenditure						
Visiting speakers						

		Notes
Transfer capital income to capital budget		This becomes 'Income' in the capital budget
Total discretionary cash outflow		
Surplus/(shortfall) income over expenditure		Operating income and expenditure—aim for zero. May include several restricted accounts
Gross cash outflow		Equal gross income including capital expenditure
Capital budget		
Capital income from above		
Depreciation from last year		Optional
Total available for capital projects		
Capital expenditure		
Building addition?		These items will differ for all churches
New bus?		
Any other capital items required by the church		
Total capital expenditure		

APPENDIX 2. REMUNERATION POLICY

Model evangelical church: Policy for remuneration and allowances paid to employees

1. General

All pastors and other workers who reduce their opportunity to earn income because of their service to the church may have their income supplemented or fully paid by the church, thereby becoming employees. In all cases, the combined income from all sources must not exceed that which would be paid if the employee were fully employed by the church in accordance with this policy. The terms applicable to all employees shall be the greater of this policy or applicable statutory rights.

The entire policy must be applied by a remuneration committee comprising at least one elder, the treasurer and at least one deacon, preferably none of whom should be an employee.

Part-time employees may be paid in one of the following two ways:

1.1. By paying the difference between the gross income which would have been paid if the worker were full–time and the gross income actually received from other sources, or

1.2. By paying per hour for a typical employee doing similar work in secular employment.

1.3. Visiting preachers are to be treated in accordance with this policy, with their preaching fee being based on the salary that would be paid to a full-time pastor minus the fringe benefits, except that he shall also be paid for his travel costs.

1.4. The church may employ the pastor's wife to act as his secretary and answer his phone, etc., either directly or by splitting some of the pastor's remuneration with his wife. The principles of this policy shall apply to her as well but special care must be exercised in order not to infringe any tax laws.

2. Leave

2.1. Ordinary and long leave must be treated as follows:

2.1.1. Pastors will be given 28 calendar days' (including 4 Sundays) ordinary leave plus 14 calendar days' long leave per annum. The long leave is to compensate for the longer working week and may be accumulated and taken at one time as a 'sabbatical'.

2.1.2. All other employees will be given 28 calendar days' ordinary leave only.

2.1.3. At the resignation of an employee, only the balance of any current leave to a maximum of one full year's allowance will be paid out. No leave will be allowed during any notice period. In the event of death in service or at retirement the elders and the remuneration committee must recommend to the church a reasonable payout of leave to the pastor's estate, taking length of service and contribution over the years into account.

2.1.4. Ordinary leave not exceeding 5 days may be taken with the consent of a designated officer (e.g. the secretary or an elder). Leave in excess of 5 days must be approved in advance by the remuneration committee and reported to the church.

2.2. Disability or sick leave may be granted by the remuneration committee for a continuous period of up to 90 days per 12-month cycle, but longer periods require the approval of the church on the recommendation of the remuneration committee and of the elders.

2.3. Official leave. This is absence from normal duties with the consent or backing of the church. It typically occurs when another organization seeks the services of the worker or pastor and the church endorses the absence. In this case, the absence shall not be deducted from leave.

2.4. Payments made to employees for services rendered during ordinary or long leave may be retained by the worker or pastor. Payments to a pastor or worker during official leave (as defined in 2.3 above), or during normal working hours, shall be paid over to the church.

2.5. Genuine gifts made by individuals or organizations to a pastor or worker may be retained by the employee.

3. Time off

Employees should generally follow normal office hours: 40 hours over a 5-day week. Pastors will inevitably work irregular and longer hours, but are expected to be diligent and available. It is, however, mandatory that they take one day off per week (not on leave) from church duties. The elders are to ensure that others are available to perform their functions on these days. In addition, most of Saturday is to be left free for the pastor to spend time with his family and on any final preparation for the Lord's Day.

4. Salary and allowances

The total package paid to any employee must be adequate to maintain a standard of living comparable with the typical members of the church in a similar occupation. For example, in the case of the pastor, a similar occupation may be that of a teacher. Packages must be reviewed annually.

Either of the following alternatives may be followed under this section:

Case 1: Needs plus contribution

The basic principle underlying remuneration is to pay in accordance with both needs and contribution to some degree. Salary is to be calculated as follows:

4.1. A basic salary. Let this be 100 units for a pastor, 85 for an associate, 72 for a worker, 60 for a secretary, or however many units the remuneration committee decides. These units should not be altered frequently.

4.2. Add an additional 30% for a wife and each dependant over 16 years of age to a maximum of …

4.3. Add an additional 15% for each dependant under 16 years of age to a maximum of 2.

4.4. Add an additional 2% for each year of appropriate service, to a maximum of 10 years.

4.5. Add an additional 10% for the first appropriate qualification; add 5% for each additional qualification. (An allowable qualification is broadly taken to be a degree for a pastor and a secretarial diploma for a secretary.)

4.6. Round up to the nearest unit.

Case 2: Benchmarks

In this case, an acceptable benchmark may be adopted and applied automatically each year. In the UK, this could be the FIEC recommendations, and in other countries, it could be the national pay scales for teachers, university lecturers or whatever profession represents a 'typical' church member.

5. Fringe benefits

5.1. Pastors' housing. It is the policy of the church to provide each pastor with a dwelling, preferably assisting him to acquire his own dwelling. This is to be accomplished as follows:

5.1.1. Make a loan to each pastor to permit him to pay the deposit on his house (see 5.2 below), and

5.1.2. Pay an accommodation allowance equal to the interest payable to a mortgage provider on the initial value of the loan plus a predetermined value to cover the cost of taxes and utilities, or

5.1.3. Pay the full rental, including taxes and utilities, on a rented house.

5.2. Loan to pastors. The church may make an interest-free loan to each pastor not exceeding twice his gross annual basic salary. Such a loan may be used to acquire a car, pay the deposit on a house, buy capital goods, etc. This loan shall be repaid at a rate of at least 1% of the original loan per month. As this is a related-party transaction, legal advice must be taken to ensure adherence to the law.

5.3. Employee pension. The church will pay into a retirement fund up to 15% of the gross income as defined in clause 4.6 by subscribing on behalf of the employee to a fund of his/her choice.

5.4. Medical insurance. The church will pay all the contributions to a medical insurance (not required in some countries, but a top-up plan may be advisable).

5.5. Car allowance. The church will assist each pastor to acquire his own vehicle and will pay an allowance which is reasonable to cover the proportion of the car's total expenses that are incurred on behalf of the church.

5.6. Book allowance. The church will pay for books and periodicals consistent with the ministry of each pastor. An amount is to be determined each year by the remuneration committee.

5.7. Telephone allowance. The church will pay the fixed line rental for a landline and one mobile phone for any employee who makes significant use of a telephone, provided that he/she makes these numbers available to the congregation. The church will also reimburse the employee for reasonable telephone use for church

activities up to a maximum amount determined each
year by the remuneration committee.

5.8. Pastors' hospitality allowance. The church will pay a
hospitality allowance to each pastor adequate to cover
all church-related hospitality. (For tax purposes, the
pastor may need to record the names of all people
receiving hospitality.)

5.9. Heating and lighting. To the extent allowed by taxation,
an allowance may be paid to the pastor or worker for
heating and lighting, provided that his or her home is
used by church members.

5.10. Use of home. In the event that the pastor or worker owns
his or her house and uses some if it for church-related
work, the church may pay rental for this use. Such rental
may be taxable in the pastor or worker's hands, but
interest and other costs may be offset against this
income.

5.11. Insurance. The church will insure employees against
accidental death for an amount equal to at least twice
their gross annual salary as defined in clause 4.6.

Note 1. All or any of the above allowances may be paid to
church employees as the remuneration committee deem fit.

Note 2. Tax. The remuneration committee should consult
people knowledgeable about tax matters to ensure that this
policy is tax efficient and does not breach any tax laws.

6. Extra church activities

No employee of the church should be involved in any activity
which:

6.1. Consumes significant time in excess of the day off and
Saturdays.

6.2. Results in financial gain to the employee, unless this is
declared to the church in accordance with clause 1.

6.3. Is in conflict with the aims of the church.

In the event of an employee wishing to embark on any significant non-church activity (such as writing a book) which does not contravene the above conditions, he/she may request permission of the church and such permission shall not be unreasonably withheld. In this case, the proceeds of the activity may be retained by the employee.

7. Copyright

All work performed by any employee of the church (except where specially excluded, such as in the writing of a book) shall be the property of the church. Copyright shall, therefore, automatically be the property of the church and may be recorded, copied, distributed free or sold with the proceeds going to the church.

8. Resignation and notice

Pastors shall disclose to the elders of the church all calls that are extended to them so that they can join them in praying for guidance. The normal notice period for all pastors is 3 calendar months from both parties. Pastors should not resign their office without good reason and the resignation should be approved by the church before it becomes effective.

The normal notice period of all other employees is 1 calendar month.

FOR FURTHER HELP AND INFORMATION

Churches' Handbook (Fellowship of Independent Evangelical Churches, April 2006). This is a UK publication for FIEC churches that contains much helpful information.

The US-based Crown Financial Ministries offer all of the works of Larry Burkett as well as many other articles and books on finance. In particular, they have produced a series of articles on stewardship in the church with views similar to those expressed in this book. American readers will find the US-specific advice of particular value. Visit http://www.crown.org/library/

http://www.apuritansmind.com—this website contains resources which cover many areas of church life.

ENDNOTES

1 http://www.apuritansmind.com/Stewardship/StewardMainPage.htm (accessed July 2008).

2 C. H. Spurgeon, *Spurgeon's Devotional Bible: Selected Passages From the Word of God with Running Comments* (Darlington: Evangelical Press, 1995), p. 366.

3 See, for example, Mark E. Dever, *Nine Marks of a Healthy Church* (Washington: Center for Church Reform, 1998). While I do not fully agree with Mark Dever's view of deacons, this is a useful and concise book.

4 For a sensitive exposition of 1 Corinthians 9:1–14, see Chapter 6 of Mark Dever, *Twelve Challenges Churches Face* (Wheaton, IL: Crossway, 2008).

5 Derek Prime and Alistair Begg, *On Being a Pastor* (Chicago, IL: Moody Publishers, 2004).

6 Larry Burkett wrote over sixty books on finance. See, for example, *Family Budget Workbook* (Chicago, IL: Moody Publishers, 1993).

About Day One:

Day One's threefold commitment:
- To be faithful to the Bible, God's inerrant, infallible Word;
- To be relevant to our modern generation;
- To be excellent in our publication standards.

I continue to be thankful for the publications of Day One. They are biblical; they have sound theology; and they are relevant to the issues at hand. The material is condensed and manageable while, at the same time, being complete—a challenging balance to find. We are happy in our ministry to make use of these excellent publications.

JOHN MACARTHUR, PASTOR-TEACHER, GRACE COMMUNITY CHURCH, CALIFORNIA

It is a great encouragement to see Day One making such excellent progress. Their publications are always biblical, accessible and attractively produced, with no compromise on quality. Long may their progress continue and increase!

JOHN BLANCHARD, AUTHOR, EVANGELIST AND APOLOGIST

Visit our web site for more information and
to request a free catalogue of our books.

www.dayone.co.uk

Also available

Look after your voice
Taking care of the preacher's greatest asset

MIKE MELLOR

96PP, PAPERBACK

ISBN 978-1-84625-125-2

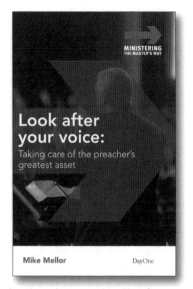

'As a hammer is to a carpenter, a scalpel to a surgeon, a trowel to a brick mason or a needle to a tailor—so the voice is to a preacher. Man's voice is the primary means God uses to deliver His Word to mankind, yet how often we who are called to impart the most important truths in the world are apt to neglect, if not wilfully abuse our all-vital 'tool of the trade'. Can there be any more pitiful sight in all nature than a God-sent preacher who is forced to be silent? We are not thinking here however of a silence brought about by pressure from ungodly sources, but that which has been enforced because of the preacher's own negligence concerning his voice. Mike Mellor's goal is not to produce another speech book (of which a good number can be found, usually aimed at actors or singers) but that something of our high calling as God's spokesmen may be re-kindled and as a consequence our desire to care for the frail vehicle God has designed to convey his Word may be increased.

'... I haven't seen anything like it for years, so it fits a good and helpful niche in the market ... If, like me, you are prepared to pay the social cost of conditioning your voice by compulsive 'humming', you should still buy this little volume for the serious advice it contains.'

JONATHAN STEPHEN, PRINCIPAL, WALES EVANGELICAL SCHOOL OF THEOLOGY AND DIRECTOR, AFFINITY

'In much of our modern preaching, a great deal of catching up is necessary in terms of actual effective delivery. This book by an open-air preacher will help us in our public speaking—even if our voices never have quite the resonance of a John Chrysostom, a Whitefield or a Billy Graham. I certainly intend to put into prayerful practice the invaluable suggestions and exercises given us by Mike Mellor.'

RICO TICE, CO-AUTHOR OF *CHRISTIANITY EXPLORED* AND ASSOCIATE MINISTER AT ALL SOULS CHURCH, LONDON

Also available

Discipline with care
Applying biblical correction in your church

STEPHEN MCQUOID

96PP, PAPERBACK

ISBN 978-1-84625-152-8

Discipline is one of the most difficult issues in contemporary church life. Church leaders often need to battle to maintain the integrity of their churches, sometimes with tragic results. But why is it so hard? Should we bother with it at all?

In this thorough treatment of the subject, Stephen McQuoid answers these questions and provides a biblical framework for church discipline. Because prevention is better than cure, he shows that discipline is not just about punishing but includes a whole way of life which keeps us spiritually accountable and in a right relationship with God. Corrective discipline will also at times be necessary, and he guides us through the disciplinary stages taught in the New Testament. By using appropriate case studies, he also demonstrates the complications of real-life situations and highlights the lessons that can be learned.

'Stephen McQuoid emphasises the need for leaders not to shirk the correction of members no matter how difficult. In exercising discipline the church is giving God's verdict on the given situation. There must, therefore, be both judgement and compassion. Helpful advice is given to both leaders and members as to what kind of attitude should be displayed towards the offender.'

DAVID CLARKSON, ELDER AT CARTSBRIDGE EVANGELICAL CHURCH AND AUTHOR OF 'LEARNING TO LEAD' COURSE

'In any local church, the issues of authority, discipline and leadership lie close to the surface. Stephen's book explores succinctly some of the cultural issues, scriptural context and practical outworkings of the vital need to keep the body in shape.'

ANDREW LACEY, CHURCH ELDER, MANAGER GLO BOOK SHOP, DIRECTOR OF PARTNERSHIP, SCOTLAND

Coming soon

Visit the sick
Shepherding the afflicted and dying in your congregation

BRIAN CROFT

96PP, PAPERBACK

ISBN 978-1-84625-143-6

The demands of the twenty-first-century have led to the neglect of certain essential responsibilities in the life of a Christian. One of those is the visitation and care of the sick in our congregations. This book is designed to instruct and motivate pastors, church leaders, and other care-giving Christians through the counsel of our heroes of church history, to recapture the practice of visiting the sick. This is accomplished by considering three specific areas. First, is our commitment to the theological as we consider how to most effectively care for their souls. Second, is our commitment to the pastoral, which instructs us how to proceed with wisdom and discernment in the variety of circumstances we will face. Third, is our commitment to the practical so that the manner in which we care for the sick will help, not hinder our effort to communicate biblical truth to them.

'Many younger pastors (and not so young ones as well) have never received the sort of very practical guidance which Brian Croft gives in this book. It will now be a recommended text in my Pastoral Ministries class.'

RAY VAN NESTE, PH.D., ASSOCIATE PROFESSOR OF CHRISTIAN STUDIES, DIRECTOR, R. C. RYAN CENTER FOR BIBLICAL STUDIES, UNION UNIVERSITY, ELDER, CORNERSTONE COMMUNITY CHURCH

'Church member, let this book equip you to become more useful to those in your church who are ailing. Young pastor, gain from Brian's practical wisdom. Seasoned pastor, let this book remind you of the privilege it is to serve and encourage the sick in a fallen world. I plan to read it together with our elders, and hope to make it available to our congregation as an equipping tool.'

PAUL ALEXANDER, SENIOR PASTOR, FOX VALLEY BIBLE CHURCH, ST. CHARLES, IL, CO-AUTHOR, THE DELIBERATE CHURCH